I0811203

CORE LIBRARY OF US STATES

MAINE

BY HANNAH PERKINS

CONTENT CONSULTANT
Tilly Laskey
Curator, Maquoit Museum Solutions

Core Library

An Imprint of Abdo Publishing
abdobooks.com

abdobooks.com

Published by Abdo Publishing, a division of ABDO, PO Box 398166, Minneapolis, Minnesota 55439.
Copyright © 2023 by Abdo Consulting Group, Inc. International copyrights reserved in all countries. No part of this book may be reproduced in any form without written permission from the publisher. Core Library™ is a trademark and logo of Abdo Publishing.

Printed in the United States of America, North Mankato, Minnesota.
052022
092022

THIS BOOK CONTAINS RECYCLED MATERIALS

Cover Photo: Shutterstock Images
Interior Photos: Sean Pavone/Shutterstock Images, 4–5, 43; Red Line Editorial, 9 (Maine), 9 (USA); Brianna Soukup/Portland Press Herald/Getty Images, 10–11; Kristin Castenschiold/Shutterstock Images, 13; Comet Design/Shutterstock Images, 17 (flag); Richard Seeley/Shutterstock Images, 17 (moose); Shutterstock Images, 17 (bird), 26–27, 45; Denis Nata/Shutterstock Images, 17 (cat); Boyd J. English/Shutterstock Images, 17 (pine cone); Brittany Courville/Shutterstock Images, 20–21; Mihai Andritoiu/Shutterstock Images, 23; Brianna Soukup/Portland Press Herald/Getty Images, 25; Bruce Peter/Shutterstock Images, 29; James Kirkikis/Shutterstock Images, 31; Thomas J. McLaughlin/Shutterstock Images, 32; Gabe Souza/Portland Press Herald/Getty Images, 34–35; Romiana Lee/Shutterstock Images, 39

Editor: Marie Pearson
Series Designer: Joshua Olson

Library of Congress Control Number: 2021951399

Publisher's Cataloging-in-Publication Data

Names: Perkins, Hannah, author.
Title: Maine / by Hannah Perkins
Description: Minneapolis, Minnesota : Abdo Publishing, 2023 | Series: Core library of US states | Includes online resources and index.
Identifiers: ISBN 9781532197604 (lib. bdg.) | ISBN 9781098270360 (ebook)
Subjects: LCSH: U.S. states--Juvenile literature. | Northeastern States--Juvenile literature. | Maine--History--Juvenile literature. | Physical geography--United States--Juvenile literature.
Classification: DDC 974.1--dc23

Population demographics broken down by race and ethnicity come from the 2019 census estimate. Population totals come from the 2020 census.

CONTENTS

CHAPTER ONE

THE PINE TREE STATE

Visitors line up outside the Portland Head Light on a warm September morning. A light breeze carries the sharp scent of salty air. The lighthouse is the oldest in Maine. It has guided sailors into Portland Harbor since it was first lit in 1791.

Climbing to the top of the lighthouse is something few visitors get to do. The only day of the year it is allowed is on Open Lighthouse Day each September. The town of Cape Elizabeth sells just 280 tickets for this

The Portland Head Light was commissioned by President George Washington.

special event. The lucky ticket holders get to go inside and scale the steep, winding staircase all the way to the giant light at the top. The view is spectacular in every direction. Toward the sea they see the white-capped waves of the Atlantic Ocean rolling toward the rocky coastline. Looking inland, they see pine trees stretching out for miles. Maine is nicknamed the Pine Tree State because of these forests.

LIGHTHOUSES GALORE

A total of 65 lighthouses line Maine's coast. The easternmost is West Quoddy Head Light in Lubec. It is part of Quoddy Head State Park. The lighthouse is also on the easternmost point in the United States. People who arrive before sunrise get to be the very first in the country to see the sun that day. Wabanaki, the name the Native people use for themselves and their homelands, means "People of the Dawn" because they are the first to see the sunrise.

WHERE IS MAINE?

What is currently Maine has long been home to the Wabanaki people. Today Maine is the farthest northeast

US state. It's part of the New England region.

Maine is the only US state to be bordered by just one other state. New Hampshire lies to both the west and south of Maine. Canada borders Maine to the northwest, north, and northeast. The Atlantic Ocean is to the state's southeast. Because of the many inlets and bays, Maine has 3,478 miles (5,597 km) of coastline. This is even more than California has.

PERSPECTIVES

A SACRED SPACE

The mountain Katahdin is the highest point in Maine. It is a sacred place for Wabanaki people. In the Penobscot language, the name Katahdin (Ktàtən) means "the greatest mountain." Many Penobscot people make an annual journey to the mountain to honor their connection to their ancestors. The land and the nearby Penobscot River are also a big part of daily life for the nation. Penobscot Nation natural resources director John Banks has said, "It's home to native brook trout, spawning salmon, white-tailed deer, and moose. It provides sustenance through the seasons for many tribal families."

Maine offers many cities and attractions. Portland is the largest city. It is a center for business and tourism. Augusta is the state capital. One historic site people often visit is Old Fort Western. This wooden fort was built before the Revolutionary War (1775–1783). Eastport was an important location during the War of 1812 (1812–1815). This war played a role in Maine's becoming a state in 1820. The bloodless Aroostook War took place in Fort Kent in 1839. This conflict helped set the boundary between Maine and Canada.

Mount Desert Island is Maine's largest island. It is home to Acadia National Park. Visitors there enjoy outdoor activities such as hiking and camping. Many dine on fresh lobster or blueberry pie before leaving. On Monhegan Island, visitors can see seals swimming nearby. Some tourists stay in bed-and-breakfast hotels. Others explore a shipwreck. Each island is unique.

MAP OF
MAINE

Look closely at this map of Maine. How does it help you understand the information in Chapter One?

CHAPTER TWO

HISTORY OF MAINE

Wabanaki people have lived in Maine for at least 13,000 years according to the archaeological record and from time immemorial according to their creation histories. The Wabanaki Confederacy includes five communities: the Abenaki, Maliseet, Micmac, Passamaquoddy, and Penobscot nations. The Maliseet (Wəlastəkwewiyik) Nation, Passamaquoddy (Peskotomuhkati) Nation, and Micmac (Mi'kmaq) Nation have communities near the

The Abbe Museum in Bar Harbor teaches visitors about the Wabanaki's presence in Maine, both past and present.

Canada border. Each has tribes across the border in Canada too. The Penobscot (Panawahpskewtək^{w}) Nation is based on Indian Island in the Penobscot River. The Abenaki are based in western Maine along the Sandy and Androscoggin Rivers. Historically, the waterways served as highways for Wabanaki people, because they traveled mainly by canoe.

Each season in the state is very different. But Wabanaki people learned how to make the most of each one. In spring they planted corn along riverbanks. Summer meant fishing and picking ripe berries. By fall, the corn was ready to harvest. In winter the Wabanaki peoples hunted land animals in the woods.

This way of life worked well for the Wabanaki peoples until European settlers arrived in the region. The Europeans broke the treaties and agreements they made with the Wabanaki peoples and claimed the land and resources for themselves. Areas that the Wabanaki people had once traveled were blocked with houses,

Beginning in the 1600s, beaver fur was a valuable product for American Indian peoples to trade with Europeans.

fences, and dams. Wabanaki people still affirm their rights to the land and waters today.

EUROPEAN SETTLEMENT

The first French settlement was on Saint Croix Island in 1604. Also in the early 1600s, English settlers arrived. They formed a colony called the Province of Maine. The settlers hoped to make a profit off the area's furs, fish, and timber. Europeans built fisheries on the coast. They made fur trade deals with the Wabanaki. The Wabanaki traded beaver furs for metal tools and other goods.

However, as more Europeans arrived, tensions grew. Many American Indians died of

LOGGING FOR ENGLAND

By the 1600s England had cut down most of its own forests. But the country still needed timber for building masts for wooden ships and to support lumber mills. England looked to the American colonies to fill this need. It declared the largest white pine trees of Maine the property of the king of England. Most of these trees had been cut down by the start of the Revolutionary War.

European diseases. Wabanaki peoples continued to assert their right to use land for hunting, fishing, and planting through treaties, which reserved lands. But the Europeans repeatedly refused to honor the treaties.

STATEHOOD

The Province of Maine became part of the British colony of Massachusetts in 1691. By this time Maine's population included European settlers, enslaved Black people, and Wabanaki people, who were resisting settlements in their homelands. Some legal struggles over land continue today in the Maine court system.

The American colonies gained their independence from the British in the Revolutionary War (1775–1783). The year the war ended, Massachusetts made slavery illegal. This law applied to what is now Maine as well. Colonies began entering the new country as states. The people of Maine wanted to break away from Massachusetts to become a separate state. The Massachusetts State Legislature agreed to allow Maine statehood in 1819. The move angered many people in the South, where slavery was legal. Southerners saw a new northern state as a threat to their ability to keep people enslaved. Many northern states wanted to end slavery throughout the country. But the southern states did not. They worried about being outnumbered if the states voted on the issue in Congress.

Congress decided to let Missouri become a state as well. Missouri would allow slavery. That way there would still be the same number of slave states and free states. Many people in Maine were angry that their statehood was linked to statehood for a slave state.

But on March 15, 1820, Maine became the twenty-third US state. At first, the young state's economy depended in part on granite and limestone mining. Maine could easily ship those building materials to other states along the coast. By the 1880s the state mined more resources. These included slate, iron, silver, and copper.

Maine's economy continued to rely on natural resources. In 1909 lumber production peaked. Maine's forests provided wood for products such as building materials. By the mid-1900s, Maine's mining grew to include sand, gravel, clay, mica, and more metals. In the late 1900s and early 2000s, more people moved to Maine's southern cities. Some of these people came from central and northern Maine. Others moved from outside the state. The areas near the coast became especially popular. In addition to the beautiful views, the region had many job opportunities in fish packaging, canning facilities, and paper and textile mills. Although paper mills are now struggling to survive in Maine, other businesses are thriving.

MAINE
QUICK FACTS

Look at Maine's state symbols. Why do you think each is important to the state?

Abbreviation: ME
Nickname: The Pine Tree State
Motto: *Dirigo* (I direct)
Date of statehood: March 15, 1820
Capital: Augusta
Population: 1,362,359
Area: 35,380 square miles (91,634 sq km)

STATE SYMBOLS

State animal
Moose

State cat
Maine coon cat

State bird
Black-capped chickadee

State flower
White pine cone and tassel

PERSPECTIVES

MAINE'S FIRST FEMALE SENATOR

When Margaret Chase Smith's husband, Clyde, died in 1940, she replaced him in the US House of Representatives. She then ran for election in the next term and won. In 1949 she became Maine's first female senator and the first woman to serve in both the House and Senate. She ran for president in 1964, but she did not win. Smith's parents were working-class people. She didn't go to college. Before entering politics, she worked as a telephone operator. Journalist Peggy Noonan wrote, "She was proud of all this and liked to speak of her roots, not to brag about her steep climb but as a kind of affirmation: Look what's possible in America."

GOVERNMENT

Today Maine's government has three branches. The executive branch is led by the governor. The legislative branch of senators and representatives makes laws. The judicial branch is the court system, which enforces laws.

Thousands of American Indians still live in Maine. There are four federally recognized tribes in the state. They are the Aroostook Band of

Micmac Indians, the Houlton Band of Maliseet Indians, the Passamaquoddy Tribe, and the Penobscot Nation. The Abenaki are not federally recognized. Tribes govern themselves. A tribal ambassador from the Penobscot Nation and a leader from the Passamaquoddy Tribe are part of Maine's legislative branch. However, they are not allowed to vote on bills. And in the past, the Wabanaki weren't allowed to vote in elections. Maine kept them from voting in federal elections until 1954. And it did not let them vote in state elections until 1967.

FURTHER EVIDENCE

Chapter Two discusses Maine's history. What was one of the main points and its supporting evidence? Read the article at the website below. Does the information on the website support this point? Does it present new evidence?

HISTORY

abdocorelibrary.com/maine

CHAPTER THREE

GEOGRAPHY AND CLIMATE

Maine is known for its mountains and ocean shoreline. The state's cool, wet climate determines what plants and animals can survive there. In the winter Maine usually gets 50 to 70 inches (127–178 cm) of snow.

More than 10,000 years ago, glaciers covered what is now Maine. The glaciers slowly scraped along the ground. They left behind sand and gravel. Today the western side of the state is rugged. High peaks are separated by

The mountain Katahdin is in Baxter State Park.

narrow valleys and lakes. The Appalachian mountain chain's northernmost point is in west-central Maine.

Rolling hills make up the south and central regions. Rivers flow through the state. The longest is the Saint John River. It flows through both Maine and Canada. Forests cover more than 89 percent of Maine's land. Oak, spruce, fir, and pine trees are some of the most common trees.

PERSPECTIVES

THE BIGGEST LAKES IN MAINE

Moosehead Lake is the largest lake in both Maine and New England. It measures 120 square miles (310 sq km). This lake has a wooded bluff. Visitors often spot wildlife such as moose and deer from this location. Sebago Lake is the deepest and second-largest lake in Maine. It is 316 feet (96 m) deep at its deepest point. Sebago's beaches are lined with tall pine trees. Their root systems extend from the sand like giant crab legs.

ANIMALS AND PLANTS

The east coast of Maine is sandy and rocky. Thousands of tiny islands lie off the mainland. People live on

Wetlands in Maine are important habitats for migratory birds.

some of them. Others contain only plant and animal life. Still others are simply rocky cliffs. Many animals live in the ocean. These include seals, lobsters, shrimp, clams, and Atlantic salmon.

Maine also has a variety of wetlands. There are marshes, wooded swamps, and thousands of lakes and ponds. The marshes near the coast help with flooding. They take in waves from the ocean. This slows down rushing waters, keeping them from eroding the land. Swamps and lakes are key habitats for wildlife.

Some birds, such as great blue herons, feed along the coast of the ocean as well as along rivers and ponds.

Maine's plants and animals have adapted to live in cold and wet climates. Furry mammals such as beavers live in the state. Some of the largest moose and black bear populations in the country are in Maine. The fur of these animals becomes thicker in winter to keep them warm. Other mammals such as whales live in the ocean. They have layers of fat called blubber to stay warm.

MASSIVE ANIMALS

Moose and whales are two large mammals that live in Maine. So many moose live in the forests that one photographer spotted 72 in just two hours. During spring, summer, and fall, humpback whales swim near the Gulf of Maine. They are known for flipping their tails when they dive. Minke whales swim closer to shore.

NOR'EASTERS

Maine is not as prone to many of the natural disasters that are common in other parts of the United States. Hurricanes, tornadoes, and large earthquakes

People in Maine may need to dig out their cars after snowstorms.

are rare. But nor'easters, or northeasters, happen often in the state. These strong winter storms bring high levels of rain and snow. They also have strong winds that come from the northeast and give the storms their name.

EXPLORE ONLINE

Chapter Three discusses nor'easters. The website below focuses on the same topic. As you know, every source is different. How is the information at the website different from the information in this chapter? What information is the same? What information did you learn from the website?

WHAT IS A NOR'EASTER?

abdocorelibrary.com/maine

19NRV
DIFFERENT APPROACH
PORTLAND, MAINE

CHAPTER FOUR

RESOURCES AND ECONOMY

Because Maine is located on the ocean, it is famous for seafood, especially lobster. In the 2010s local fishers brought in record numbers of lobster. They often caught more than 120 million pounds (54 million kg) in a year. But fishing isn't the largest part of Maine's economy. The largest part is service jobs. These include health-care and transportation jobs. Maine has railroads, airports, highways, and ferries.

Some lobster boats dock in Portland.

MAINE MAPLE SYRUP

Maine is one of the top US states for producing maple syrup. Processing maple syrup comes from American Indian traditional scientific knowledge. Businesses called sugar houses produce more than 575,000 gallons (2.2 million L) of the popular product each year. Sugar house workers tap maple trees for their sap. They then boil the sap, causing water to evaporate until the sap thickens into syrup. The Maine maple syrup industry adds $27 million to the Maine economy each year.

Lumber, mining, and agriculture are other key parts of Maine's economy. These industries depend on natural resources. Lumber has declined in recent years. Much of the state's forestland has been overharvested. The northeast corner of the state has good soil for growing potatoes. Maine's soil has a lot of rocks that the glaciers left behind. Mining continues in mountains and in soil near ponds. It focuses on granite, gravel,

Most of Maine's potatoes are grown in Aroostook County.

PERSPECTIVES

PAPER MILLS

Many of Maine's paper mills are struggling. Some have closed in recent years. Smartphones and other electronic devices are the biggest reason. Their popularity has caused paper sales to drop. The lower demand for paper means fewer jobs for mill workers and loggers who supply the mills with wood. Dana Doran is the executive director of Professional Logging Contractors of Maine. He said, "Our state's logging industry and the rural communities that rely on it are all now at risk due to factors beyond their control."

and sand. Some metals and gemstones such as tourmaline are also mined.

Other parts of the economy include energy and manufacturing. Rivers have hydroelectric dams. Forests provide fuel from wood. Some open lands and ocean areas are dotted with wind turbines to make electricity. Solar farms turn sunlight into electricity. Maine factories produce items such as paper products and transportation equipment.

People enjoy the beach and amusement park at Old Orchard Beach.

MAINE TOURISM

Maine's unofficial nickname is Vacationland. The phrase has been the slogan on most Maine license plates since 1936. This is because the state draws millions of tourists each year. In 2020 Maine scored the fourth-place spot on travel publisher Lonely Planet's Top Regions list.

A wide variety of sites and seasonal fun draw visitors to Maine. In the summer the town of Old Orchard Beach swells from about 9,000 people to more than 75,000. The beach itself is 7 miles (11 km) long. In the center is a 500-foot (152-m) pier featuring shops and live entertainment at night. Families flock to

Maine has many popular ski resorts, including Shawnee Peak.

Palace Playland, an amusement park next to the beach. Fall and winter also draw visitors to Maine. The state has some of the best fall foliage in the country. Trees turn brilliant colors. The Sugarloaf, Sunday River, and Saddleback ski resorts offer some of the best skiing in the state. All of these businesses contribute to Maine's tourist economy.

STRAIGHT TO THE SOURCE

Sam Rosen grew up on the island of Vinalhaven off the coast of Maine, where he now works catching lobsters. He described growing up on the island:

> *For most people on the island, regardless of gender, if you have a parent that runs or works on a boat, it's likely that you'll spend some amount of your childhood working with them. . . . You get to play with fish and crash around in a boat all day. In my case, my dad had me hauling a few traps from the time I was 4 or 5 years old. Then you work your way up to more traps as you get older, and eventually get your own boat. For me, my dad built me a boat when I was 11 or 12.*

Source: Jeremy Venook. "Consider the Lobsterman." *Atlantic*, 28 Oct. 2016, theatlantic.com. Accessed 6 Aug. 2021.

BACK IT UP

The author of this passage is using evidence to support a point. Write a paragraph describing the point the author is making. Then write down two or three pieces of evidence the author uses to make the point.

CHAPTER FIVE

PEOPLE AND PLACES

More than 1.3 million people live in Maine. White people who are not Hispanic or Latino make up 93 percent of the population. Many of these are of French, French-Canadian, English, Italian, or Irish descent. Black, Hispanic, Asian, and American Indian people, as well as people of other racial and ethnic groups, also live in the state. Nearly 75 percent of the population lives in southwest Maine.

In the 2010s, the Passamaquoddy at Pleasant Point began work to become self-sustaining for food by tending a 167-acre (68-ha) garden.

The Black community in Maine has had a presence since the 1670s. Some were enslaved. Others worked in every aspect of the Maine economy, from dock workers to priests. In the mid-1800s, large numbers of French-Canadian and Irish immigrants came to the area. They sought work in the booming mill towns of Auburn, Biddeford, Lewiston, and Portland. About 40 years later, immigrants from Armenia, Albania, and Italy also came to the region. They worked in the textile mills and granite quarries.

The influence of the Wabanaki nations' original languages is seen throughout Maine in place names. Examples include the city of Saco, the Presumpscot River, and Monhegan Island. Canoes, snowshoes, and toboggans were used for travel and are now commonly used for recreation. These were invented by American Indians long before Europeans arrived.

Maine was also a stop on the Underground Railroad, which helped Black people escape slavery.

One such stop was the Abyssinian Meeting House in Portland. Built in 1828, it is the country's third-oldest standing Black community meeting house and church.

Many notable people have roots in Maine. Actress Victoria Rowell grew up in Maine. She has won 11 NAACP Image Awards for acting in a daytime TV drama. Actress and singer Anna Kendrick grew up in Portland. Actor Patrick Dempsey was born in Lewiston. Olympic marathon runner and gold medalist Joan Benoit Samuelson grew up in Cape Elizabeth.

KING OF HORROR

Best-selling author Stephen King was born in Portland. He has lived in Bangor for much of his life. He received his English degree from the University of Maine at Orono in 1970. Since that time he has become one of the world's most famous horror writers. He has written more than 60 books. Many of them have also become popular movies and television miniseries.

ACTIVITIES

Maine's natural beauty attracts many visitors. Acadia National Park is one of the ten most-visited parks in the United States. The park is on the northeast coast. It has mountains, forests, and sandy beaches. People can enjoy hiking in many landscapes there. Acadia is only one of Maine's more than 100 national and state parks and sites.

Tourists and residents alike enjoy shopping for outdoor gear and clothing at the L.L.Bean flagship store in Freeport. Leon Leonwood Bean founded the company in Maine in 1912. The company has since opened stores in many other states.

People can visit the Penobscot Nation Museum. This museum is filled with cultural artifacts and exhibits on the life of the people through history. Visitors can also arrange educational tours of Penobscot lands. The Northern Maine Fair takes place in August in the town of Presque Isle. It draws thousands of visitors and features animals, agriculture, horse shows, and truck pulls.

People enjoy the beauty of Acadia National Park.

Historic colonial and Victorian homes can be seen throughout Maine. Some were first built by early European colonists and date back as far as the 1600s. Today a handful of these homes are museums that people can visit to learn about how Maine has changed throughout the years.

Maine's seafood restaurants draw big crowds. In Portland a large floating restaurant named DiMillo's on

PERSPECTIVES

BASKET WEAVER

Jeremy Frey is a Passamaquoddy artist from Maine. In 2011 he became the second person to win best of show at both the Santa Fe Indian Market in New Mexico and the Heard Indian Market in Arizona. In 2015 Frey repeated these wins. His family has woven baskets for generations. Frey uses material from ash trees to weave his fancy baskets. But this material has become harder to find due to a pest called the emerald ash borer beetle, which kills the trees. Frey thinks his generation may be the last to use the material. "You can't replace ash for baskets," he said in an interview. "It's in our legends. It's . . . embedded in our culture."

the Water feeds hungry tourists exploring Maine's Old Port. Each July, the Yarmouth Clam Festival offers tasty food, carnival rides, and a craft fair. Northern New England's largest wooden roller coaster is in Saco at Funtown Splashtown USA. It is called Excalibur. With fun activities and natural beauty, Maine has a great deal to offer to visitors and residents alike.

STRAIGHT TO THE SOURCE

Journalist Mary Caperton Morton visited Acadia National Park. She wrote about the park for the *Guardian*:

> *Acadia was decreed the first national park in the eastern US, in 1919, and retains its elemental charm, with rugged granite cliffs, teeming tide pools and wild islands dotting the north Atlantic. Sections of the park are off-limits to cars and a network of horse-drawn carriage trails are still in use. It covers about half of Mount Desert Island, a rocky prominence of land divided into two lobes by the Somes Sound, and nearby smaller islands. . . . With a lighthouse, a campground and over 10 miles [16 km] of hiking and biking trails, this rocky island is the perfect Maine coast getaway.*

Source: Mary Caperton Morton. "Top 10 National and State Parks in New England, USA." *The Guardian*, 26 May 2015, theguardian.com. Accessed 19 Aug. 2021.

WHAT'S THE BIG IDEA?

Take a close look at Morton's words. What is her main idea? What evidence is used to support her point? Write a few sentences showing how Morton uses two or three pieces of evidence to support her main point.

IMPORTANT DATES

13,000 years ago
Wabanaki people live in what is now called Maine.

1600s
Europeans form settlements in Maine.

1791
The Portland Head Light is lit for the first time.

1820
Maine becomes the twenty-third US state on March 15.

Early 1900s
Immigrants from Armenia, Albania, and Italy come to Maine.

1909
Lumber production peaks.

1954

American Indians in Maine win the right to vote in federal elections after generations of being denied it. They still cannot vote in state elections until 1967.

2010s

Local fishers often catch more than 120 million pounds (54 million kg) of lobsters per year.

STOP AND THINK

Tell the Tale

Chapter One discusses a trip to Portland Head Light. Imagine that you are among the tourists who get to climb to the top of the lighthouse that day. Write 200 words about your experience. Describe what you see and hear, as well as how you feel standing at the top.

Surprise Me

Chapter Three discusses Maine's climate and wildlife. After reading this book, what two or three facts about this topic did you find most surprising? Write a few sentences about each fact. Why did you find each fact surprising?

Dig Deeper

After reading this book, what questions do you still have about Maine? With an adult's help, find a few reliable sources that can help you answer your questions. Write a paragraph about what you learned.

Take a Stand

Chapter Four discusses various industries in Maine. Make a list of each industry. Which industry is the most important to you in your daily life? Explain why in a few sentences.

GLOSSARY

adapt
to change over time to develop a feature or skill that helps an animal or plant survive

bluff
a steep bank along a body of water

colony
an area of land that is separate from but controlled by another country

commission
to officially order something to be made

economy
a place's system of goods, services, money, and jobs

erode
to wear away by the movement of wind, water, or other natural forces

glacier
a large body of ice that moves across land

immemorial
existing since before human memory, record, or tradition

immigrant
a person who moves to and lives in a new country

ONLINE RESOURCES

To learn more about Maine, visit our free resource websites below.

Core Library CONNECTION
FREE! COMMON CORE MULTIMEDIA RESOURCES

Visit **abdocorelibrary.com** or scan this QR code for free Common Core resources for teachers and students, including vetted activities, multimedia, and booklinks, for deeper subject comprehension.

Booklinks NONFICTION NETWORK
FREE! ONLINE NONFICTION RESOURCES

Visit **abdobooklinks.com** or scan this QR code for free additional online weblinks for further learning. These links are routinely monitored and updated to provide the most current information available.

LEARN MORE

Bell, Samantha S. *Exploring New England*. Abdo, 2018.

Ehman, Ashley M. *Maine: The Pine Tree State*. Cavendish Square, 2020.

Ward, Alexa. *America's National Parks*. Lonely Planet Kids, 2019.

INDEX

About the Author

Hannah Perkins has been a Maine resident all her life. She enjoys hiking and swimming in the summer and snowshoeing in the winter. She lives just outside Portland with her family but heads to Pine Point Beach in Scarborough whenever she gets the chance, regardless of the season.